D1433204

2 6 NOV 2019
SOUTHWARK LIBRARIES

SK 2638548   1

ANIMAL
Homes

The Arctic

By John Wood

BookLife

©2018
Book Life
King's Lynn
Norfolk PE30 4LS

ISBN: 978-1-78637-136-2

All rights reserved
Printed in Malaysia

Written by:
John Wood

Edited by:
Holly Duhig

Designed by:
Matt Rumbelow

A catalogue record for this book
is available from the British Library.

Photocredits: Abbreviations: l-left, r-right, b-bottom, t-top, c-centre, m-middle. Images are courtesy of Shutterstock.com. With thanks to Getty Images, Thinkstock Photo and iStockphoto. 2 - Denis Burdin, 3 - Denis Burdin, 4 - Ritesh Chandhary, 5tl - sirtravelalot, 5m - Lenar Musin, 5mr - Longjourneys, 5bl - Scott E Read, 5br - Fish Ho Hong Yun, 6 - ginger polina bublik, 7- Jamen Percy, 8- DonLand, 9 - Galyna Andrushko, 10 - outdoorsman, 11 - Amelie Koch, 12 - Incredible Arctic, 13 - Paul Reeves Photography, 14 - Karelian, 15 - Martin Hejzlar, 16 - CampCrazy Photography, 17 - Miles Away Photography, 18 - Sergey Uryadnikov, 19 - Helen Birkin, 20 - Yulia YasPe, 21 - Jan Martin Will, 22 - Jo Crebbin, 23 - Vladimir Wrangel

CONTENTS

Words that look like this can be found in the glossary on page 24.

WHAT IS A
HABITAT?

A habitat is a place where an animal lives. It provides the animal with food, shelter and everything else it needs to survive.

A Polar Bear on the Arctic Ice

There are lots of different habitats in the world. Each one is home to many different animals.

Forests

Oceans

Deserts

Mountains

Rainforests

5

WHAT IS THE ARCTIC?

The Arctic is an area around the North Pole which is very cold. It is made up of the Arctic Ocean and all the land around it.

The North Pole

The Arctic is home to many animals. In the winter, it can become too cold for some animals so they move south. This is called migration.

These are the northern lights, which sometimes appear in the Arctic sky.

ARCTIC HABITAT

Lots of Arctic animals live on the sea ice. In the cold winter, there is more sea ice. In the warmer summer, some of this ice melts or breaks away.

Sea Ice

Some animals live on land, in the Arctic tundra. There are no trees in the tundra because the ground is too cold. Only small shrubs and plants can grow.

Tundra

WALRUSES

Walruses are often found lying on the edge of the sea ice, or swimming in the Arctic Ocean. They live in big groups with hundreds of other walruses.

A Group of Walruses

Walruses are able to stay warm because of the blubber in their bodies. They need this blubber to stay warm in the cold waters.

ARCTIC TERNS

Arctic terns make their homes in the tundra. They dig nests on the ground called scrapes. This is where they look after their young.

A Scrape

Arctic terns don't live in the Arctic all year. In the winter, they migrate to Antarctica, which is in the South Pole.

Arctic terns migrate farther than any other animal.

LEMMINGS

Lemmings make their homes in underground burrows in the tundra. Their burrows are made up of lots of different tunnels all joined together.

A lemming peeks out of its hiding place.

Sometimes too many lemmings are born at the same time. When this happens, large groups of lemmings will migrate to find a new home with more food.

BELUGA WHALES

Beluga whales live in the Arctic Ocean, near the coast. They migrate south when the Arctic Ocean becomes too icy in the winter.

Beluga Whale

A group of beluga whales is called a pod. There are usually around ten whales in a pod. They talk to each other by chirping, clicking and whistling.

Pod of Beluga Whales

POLAR BEARS

Polar bears live on the Arctic ice. Their white fur makes them harder to see against the ice. This helps them sneak up on their prey.

Female polar bears make dens in the snow. This is where they raise their cubs. Polar bears usually have two cubs.

A Polar Bear Cub in Its Den

THE ARCTIC IN
DANGER

When harmful gases from cars, aeroplanes and factories go into the air, they trap heat on Earth and cause the planet to warm up. This is called global warming and it is putting Arctic animals in danger.

20

Global warming melts the sea ice in the Arctic. This makes it harder for some animals to survive. When an animal is finding it hard to survive, it is said to be endangered.

RINGED SEALS

Some types of ringed seals are endangered. Because global warming is melting the sea ice, many seals have nowhere to live and raise their young.

SIBERIAN CRANES

During the Arctic summer, Siberian cranes live in the tundra. But as the world gets warmer, the cold tundra is disappearing. This means Siberian cranes have less space to look for food.

GLOSSARY

blubber	a thick layer of fat under the skin of sea mammals, such as whales and seals
burrows	a hole or tunnel dug by an animal
coast	the area where the land meets the sea
dens	animal's homes, dug in earth or snow
endangered	when a species of animal is in danger of going extinct
gases	air-like substances that expand freely to fill any space available
prey	animals that are hunted by other animals for food
sea ice	sea water that freezes into ice, which is usually slightly salty
tundra	a cold area where trees do not grow
young	an animal's offspring

Index